DYSCALCULIA

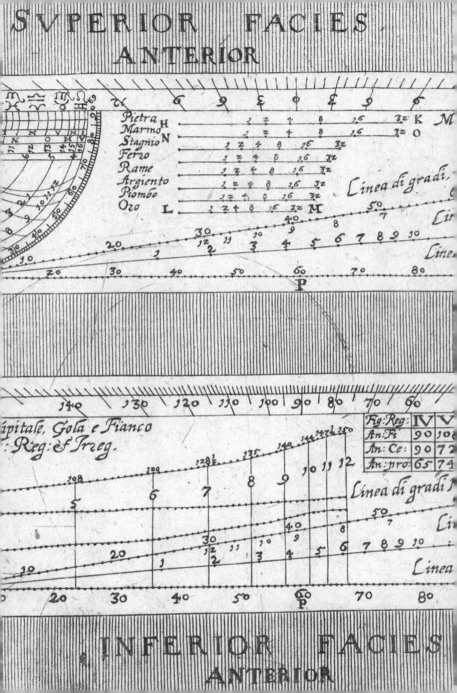

Pietra H
Marmo N
Stagnio N
Ferro
Rame
Argiento
Piombo
Oro L

Linea di gradi.

Lir

Line

P

---

140   130   120   110   100   90   80   70   60

iitale, Gola e Fianco
: Reg: e Irreg.

Fig: Reg:	IV	V
An: Fi	90	10
An: Ce:	90	72
An: pro:	65	74

108   128½   135   140   144 147 150
5   6   7   8   9   10 11 12

Linea di gradi N

Lir

30   50
12   40   40   8   7
2   11   10   9
1   2   3   4   5   6   7 8 9 10

Linea

10   20   30   40   50   60   70   80
P

DYSCALCULIA

A Love Story of Epic Miscalculation

Camonghne Felix

ONE WORLD

New York

Published in the United States by One World, an imprint of Random House,
a division of Penguin Random House LLC, New York.

ONE WORLD and colophon are registered trademarks of
Penguin Random House LLC.

Hardback ISBN 9780593242179
Ebook ISBN 9780593242186

Printed in the United States of America on acid-free paper

oneworldlit.com
randomhousebooks.com

2 4 6 8 9 7 5 3 1

First Edition

Book design by Debbie Glasserman

For anyone who's ever cried on the subway

I recognize failure—which is important; some people don't—and fix it, because it is data, it is information, knowledge of what does not work. That's rewriting.

—TONI MORRISON

dys·cal·cu·lia

/dis-ˌkal-ˈkyü-lē-ə/

noun   **PSYCHIATRY**

1. severe difficulty in making arithmetical calculations, as a result of a brain disorder

Pietra H
Marmo N
Stagnio
Ferro
Rame
Argiento
Piombo
Oro L

K M
O

1 2 4 8 16 32
1 2 4 8 16 32
1 2 4 8 16 32
1 2 4 8 16 32
1 2 4 8 16 32
1 2 4 8 16 32
1 2 4 8 16 32
1 2 4 8 16 32 M

Linea di gradi

50
40 7
30 9 8 Line
12 11 10 5 6 7 8 9 10
1 2 3 4
Line
10 20 30 40 50 60 70 80
P

140 130 120 110 100 90 80 70 60

áapitale, Gola e Fianco
Reg: ef Irreg.

Fig: Reg:	IV	V
An: Fi	90	10
An: Ce	90	7
An: pro	65	7

128 1/2 135 140 144 147 150
120 10 11 12
208
5 6 7 8 9

Linea di gradi

50
40 7
30 9 8 Li
12 11 10 5 6 7 8 9 10
1 2 3 4
Linea
10 20
0 20 30 40 50 60 70 80
P

CONTENTS

Part I

FRACTALS

As it turns out, nature has a formula that tells us
when it's an entity's time to die.

There's even an equation for it, where size becomes rule
and the laws of expiration must obey: take the mass of a
system of organisms (a species of plant, all mammals); its
metabolic rate (read: speed of entropy) is equal to its mass
taken to three-fourths power.

Pythagoreans believed that numbers were an infinite, invisible, but radically real force in an ultimate but uncreated world of exponentially dynamic beings.

They believed that numbers, and to what rhythms we assign them, give birth to the ineffable, to the faithful. This is how we learn to hear beauty, how we come to know the nature of deficits, how we know what it means to be full, what it means to offer an abundance, and how to quantify the sin of greed.

This faith is what introduces the doctrines of Plato, and through Plato, Aristotle's incarnations, and through that translation, western consciousness is born, and through western consciousness come these varying systems of order, these strange phenomena of persuasive appeal, then the Self gained a title, lending western civilization a way to feel, a way to comprehend the sequential mechanics of how each individual comes to know for certain their place and purpose in the world.

Of all artistic mediums, mine of choice is one of mathematical impulse, lyrics buoyed by the universal truth of the one and the two.

When I say I wanted to die, I do not mean it hyperbolically, metaphorically, or symbolically—I'm not trying to metaphorize an ache or insult the natural functioning of the mind. Memory makes me flawed in remembering, but this I can tell without mirage, without the phantasmagoria of misery.

One autonomous lonesome entity in a sea of other entities one day ventures out of its home, in which it dwells alone, and stumbles upon its ecological double. Bonded, the two leave their lonesome habitats and choose to reinhabit the orb of the living world as some new, mutated thing. One world, meeting another, entering another anew.

What two lovers do in the room of that third world is the math of it all.

I loved him, and it gave me a fever.

Aight, so boom:

The morning after his birthday, we lie lazy in the deep cusp of our bed, the sun's tender touch grazing the fur of our bodies. I reach over to check the time on his phone instead of mine, mostly because his was closest, mainly because a pesky impulse primed me to look and I get giddy in my ancestors' mischief. I press the phone's home button to illuminate the screen, and as if summoned, one lone text flashes white across the face: "I'm so in love with you bby, I wish you were with me last night instead of her."

At first, I smile easy at the warmth of it. I love to know the one I love is loved—a natural symptom of narcissism, or of gratitude. After a moment, a dawning flushes over me, the warm wisp of that easy morning suddenly plucked away, my pulse racing into disgust as I realize he lied, realizing I knew exactly who she was, the memory of a girl he'd curiously and opaquely befriended just a few months before projecting from my memory's drunk archives. On my birthday she offered me a shot of a dry gin, the taste of her guilt like salt on my tongue.

I had asked him. I had asked him then, and he had lied.

Like an instant high, I feel myself losing my sense of time, colors ringing in my ears, the sun brighter than ever before. I shake him awake, shaking him, shaking him.

As he wakes, I see panic fill in on his brow. "Who?" he asks. "What? I'm in love with *you,* babe, c'mon!" except the tether is missing from his eye, he is lying again, right to my face, his betrothed, his promised one.

Breathing gets difficult then, and with all the ringing in my ears, thinking is an odd task. Something takes over and I lean into my autopilot, calling Her from his phone before I even know who I'm calling. She answers, and I demand precision: I want to know what, I want to know for how long.

(Okay, tea: Apparently, he had *been planning* on leaving me. Apparently, she had been planning on waiting it out. That whole sad time, I had been planning on becoming his wife, so none of the data aligned, the margins too muddy to reconcile.)

There's silence. Then the crushing wail of a million mournings. Then a collapse. From a view above the room, I watch myself melt into a foolish rage as I'm being let in on a secret that had canceled me out, that made me the woman unwanted. All of a sudden, I am a child again, up in a flame I can't stop, an anger I can't manage.

I wanted him and I wanted him to be sorry and I wanted to be a woman who could go glamorously unaffected by such blatant ignorance, because how dare he eclipse me, make me ugly, how dare she even fucking breathe. I wanted Her ruined. I wanted Her flattened.

And I wanted to fucking die.

A fractal is a never-ending pattern—infinitely complex. It's a simple equation processed over and over again, re-producing itself in perpetuity, hiding around and inside of us, like Russian dolls, like a forest bordered by and stuffed full with trees, like a river that splits and meets itself in another river, like a stamp, like your DNA, like your brain, like your lungs, like their functions.

Where any death, even the tiniest one, is the result of a patterned agitation.

It's hurricane season. We're standing in the warm, wet Brooklyn breeze and sharing a lucky cigarette just weeks before our final dance begins, the starry lid of the sky winking down above us.

"Tinder is so weird," he tells me. "I keep starting conversations with people I can't finish."

It's like that! I tell him. *Thank god we don't* actually *have to date.*

He chuckles, taking a deep inhale on his drag of the cigarette.

I ask him: *Have you met anyone?*

I reassure him: *It's okay if you have.*

"No, of course not," he says. "You know I can't see anything but you."

The nobody of Certeau's Everyman is truly common twice: once in madness, again in death.

He is leaving the home we share for the last time, and I resist this event horizon with everything I've got, tripping as I fumble after the tail of his shirt, arms stretched long, reaching and reaching for any inch of him, him reaching for the exit, my eyes begging for him in the heavy silence of this scandalous peepshow as my two good friends look away like onlookers to a drunken scuffle, embarrassed and slightly afraid. I pull him with me into the bathroom for a bit of humble privacy, begging *just talk to me, please.* I walk him backwards into the windowless washroom, begging, begging, *please, please don't go, please look at me, I love you so much.* He lifts me by the waist, eyes as flat as the bottom of a steel pan, sits me on the bathroom sink, and enters me, one hand wrapped around my neck, one hand muffling my mouth. After three strokes he pushes himself away from me, his breathless release breaking suspension. I fall to the vinyl floor where I crumble into fetal and stay. From this corner of the universe, this single panel of cold tiled floor, I look up and the final scene begins to roll: the camera pans to the bent back of this man who once loved me pulling his pants up over his hips, then shows booted feet as he steps over me, then over the bathroom's threshold and into the corridor, then pans to his fist as it grips the knob of the front door. Finally we see his face, brown and weathered and strange. He looks down at me through a shroud of tearful, dolorous pity. He whispers, "I really am sorry, I'm so sorry," and goes.

On the other side of the freeway, traffic stalls to better observe the three-car pileup clogging the middle of the road. We slow down to get a close glimpse at the mangled metal, the twisted roofs punctuating each other with new angles and sharp lines. From where we sit, a mere twenty feet away, heads craning out of our windows, it is impossible still to know who holds ultimate fault in this tragedy, who to send the bill to. All the cars are the same color, same size, same make, 1997 white Acuras—in the end, the fault could belong to any one of them: the one distracted by her girlfriend's rage text on the way home; the one playfully racing with the station wagon in the lane next to him; the one jerking off behind the wheel. Any one of them could be the fatal other, the one with the confession to make upon meeting their maker, but regardless, in the end, even the one least responsible for the final output had the choice of the input in hand. From over here, all of the victims are villains, and all of the villains are dead.

In an article that lists "15 Crazy Instances of Self-Similarity," I see nature performing a kind of humanness. First, I evaluate whether or not what I think I see is what I see or if my human eyes assume a supremacy.

The article shows pictures of spirals in nature, in whirlpools, in sand dunes, in ringworm infections, in space. In some spirals, there is momentum and force, in others, just patterns.

When I spiral, I take on my own momentum, my own force, fractals of my many fractals taking on new diameter, echoes billowing in neon rings, sonic abstraction in the mind of a maestro.

Maybe it's an algorithm. Maybe it's me.

Sankofa in my loins, Sankofa in the meat of my memory.
I'll have to spiral back to return.

I was born smack-dab in the middle of the coldest month of the year, born bold and resistant to the unpredictable, born an urgent Sun burning a blister into the shoulder of the Earth.

Capricorn Sun, Gemini rising, Taurus Moon, Sagittarius Venus, INFP, Year of the Monkey.

"Black or White" by Michael Jackson was #1 on the *Billboard* charts the day I was born, social consciousness accepting its bifurcation, the zeitgeist setting the terms of my induction. In August of that year, Mall of America opened its doors to a new era of capitalism, and in October, Cartoon Network debuted to a generation of perpetual parodic psychosis.

Loss. Abundance. Greed.

Children see the world clearly when they first come into it. It's circumstance that sullies the walls of our terrariums, less and less light getting in each day.

The exact first time I touched a computer I can't recall,

but in the heavy-wooded armoire of my mind I can find stacks of them, every single one built by my mother, nearly from scratch—constructing motherboards memory by memory, that lockbox of formulaic intent humming with the blood of her calculated intellect.

When we were small, I watched her build them all the time, with either one of my sisters strapped to her chest, her arms bent in a bowl so as not to disturb them as she screws a power connector into its corresponding socket, Bunny Wailer wailing in the background. She caresses the enamel of the shell once built and functional, praying over it, honoring its capabilities. Only after that ritual would she install the games I wanted to play—Math Blaster!, You Can Be a Woman Engineer—collapsing the spine of the desk chair so that my eyes would rest level with the great pixelated sky of the monitor.

I was supposed to have a four-hour-a-day limit on the computer for intellectual posterity but sometimes, while my mother slept, I would creep down the short hallways from her bedroom back into mine, where the big fantastical box of formulas would await me, teasing me with the confidence of the millennium, urging me toward

Egypt where my friend Carmen Sandiego would leave clues for me, her red wings whipping in the pixeled sand.

All day, I would think about that empty computer screen and what lay behind it for me, intentionally misbehaving until someone would send me back to my room as punishment, where I could sit delighted, fixated, tantalized as the night fell down around me, the eclipsing light falling across my cheeks like an even snow.

Little by little, I begin to think in the computer's language, its pointer shaping the contours of my dreams. I was dreaming in programs and codes and colors and compounds, dreaming in trapped doors that open with modular keys, dreaming in the voices of my virtual guides, dreaming from behind the wheel of a car powered by good grammar, Mavis Beacon's wily tone lulling me to sleep, singing to me: "Good job. Are you ready for the next lesson?"

Those were the days when I loved math. I swear I did.

When I was very young, like ten or eleven, having already lost the silent right to my girlhood, I discovered the body to be a sexual body with portals and buttons that open to the heavy hand of heat. And I also discovered porn. It was when I discovered porn, slowly and precisely uncovering each corner of the cloaked web, that I discovered kink, and as I discovered kink, I discovered one immutable fact of human nature: there is something in all of us that craves the shadow side of abject humiliation.

It was second grade when I realized I was different, and it would be a tragedy.

When I was distracted, I would float high above the room, noticing everything, the way the clock ticked, how the dust on the board settled, the way the corners of the carpet frayed, how the room itself smelled, the wind from the outside wafting the spring in.

I thought to myself that the room smelled like sex. And I didn't realize what I was thinking until I'd said it out loud. My twenty-something-year-old teacher, mortified, just stares at me for a moment, because wtf. Because how horrid to hear an eight-year-old say something so ominous, so unusual. When I said it, the room gasped, children's voices aflurry, and suddenly I was back down on that alphabet rug, no longer floating, red with the humiliation of what I had said out loud.

But I knew what I knew. Like a locket, that smell was its own memory. I smelled the scent of that familiar, musky vigor, and I left my body. That was the truth. In a few moments, I'm whisked out of the classroom and into the front office, where I sit in the big leather chair next to the check-in desk as I would if I were my own parent. I can't recall what happened next.

"It's such a fuckin' old pain that, you know, there's nothing poetic about it," Fiona sings, and shit if that's not true.

There was a big fall when I was a toddler. I don't remember it at all, not even a vague sense of the injury, but my mom insists that it was awful and that I could have died. She seems so haunted by the memory that I suppress the urge to dismiss her dramatics and choose to take it at face value.

After I tell the truth about the blood in my underwear, every day seems like the day of the big, bad fall and she mentions it all the time, like it should constitute something. She mentions it whenever I'm gone and she's looking for me, her long piano fingers gripping my jaw, searching the shallow caverns of my eyes for a clue. She mentions it just before she pulls away, exhausted and demoralized. She gives up, decides she's lost me. "Remember that fall? Hmm. My little girl . . . someone took my little girl and I don't know where she went."

O, Fiona—your analysis and your precision. How you know that the job of dispossession *is* the balm to the old pain, how you know that momentum is what makes all the dark shit beautiful. I love how you know that a coat of paint is insufficient, the markings will show up anyway. They'll show up like a rag. They'll show up somewhere in this listicle of analysis, in the checkout on our way back to the car—

but not in the way we're told, and never as convenient as it should.

The need to storytell is compulsive and agnostic; unfortunately

everything I need to know about my self becomes document.

When I finally let it out, said it plain that my older cousin had been raping me, a fine transmutation occurred. Some anti-world entity swooped in, lifting me from one body and dropping me into another. Nothing was the same.

A sorrow I'd never known became my mother. My grandmother lost her smile. My dad disassociated and it burned him up from the inside out, ulcers whipping at the post. Then came my other grandmother's new skepticism, her watchful eye now stern and hardened, my skirts too short and my hips suddenly too wide. The logic of everything had been complicated beyond comprehension. I told the truth and got put on punishment, that new shame like a red stripe across my face.

On a cellular level, it confounded me that the truth could—in property and in consequence—behave the same way as a lie.

I was talking to a lawyer within twenty-four hours, and a therapist in forty-eight.

Process rolled into more process, and I was being asked to recount each assault over and over again—first for the police, then a detective, then a doctor, then a lawyer, then the associate, then, then, then. Everyone needed a granular level of detail that I hadn't yet collected prior to their asking, so every conversation was a violent unearthing, an ongoing pluck, and a prodding at the thin, wearying skin of my psyche.

Sequence in process was the first sense to go. With each retell, each new therapist, bit by bit I could feel the glitching start, my executive functions beginning to complicate. Memory was burning a hole through my capacities, taking up so much space and getting heavier and heavier, my brain's ability to process taking away from its ability to compute.

"This washcloth is dry, did you even bathe?"

"No, we've gone over this—calculate what's in the parenthesis <u>first</u>, and **then** the exponents."

Second,

first,
order,

what is?

As my functions continued to deteriorate, basic things that were once second nature became foreign—the fundamental stuff, like washing myself in the bath or remembering homework, staying awake during class or finishing tasks on time. It was hard to follow Mavis Beacon's prompts, the spelling-powered car leaving me behind in the dust.

After a few weeks of evaluation, the psychiatrist the law-
yers recommended to us recommended pharmaceutical
treatment to help preserve my executive functioning
amongst the poisonous debilitation of the PTSD. We
tried Ritalin first. I'm eight and already on drugs. It's
an irony we couldn't anticipate, my mother humming
through the cool grays of the morning as she works the
pills down my throat, holding back her own sick.

> Day one was a colorful day. Every-
> thing moved much faster and my
> body felt much warmer, the sun
> somehow following my lead.

> Day two was up and down. It was
> as if my hormones were on an axis,
> dipping in and out of my cerebel-
> lum at various levels, much too
> much, and much too little all at
> once.

Day three was an absolute blur. I slept through every class and didn't touch my lunch.

Day four was like day three.

Day twelve was like day eight.

Day twenty was like day ten.

And then all the days become the sisters of the other.

I loved Ritalin. Everything pink and putrid and rich. Hundreds of miles outside of my body, thousands of miles outside of my mind.

After two weeks like day three, my mother demanded that they find another treatment—"You said it would improve her focus but it's making it worse; she's out of it all the time"—they tell her there are no better treatments.

Mom chose to wean me off the Ritalin, inspired none by the lack of general information provided to her about the drug itself or how it might affect me long-term. I came back to the living world more irritable and angsty than I'd been before, more skeptical too, offended that I seemed to be the only one who knew that I had physically and spiritually lost time.

Time is an anarchy.

There are whole sections of years that have, in my mind, disappeared, time revealing its tricks to me like a cocky necromantic. The gaps are caverns of absence, temporal wormholes, where all I can recall is the sensation of being stretched between many different dimensions of crisis at once.

Off meds and progress in talk therapy plateauing, I'm left to process my penance alone, up at odd hours of the night replaying my cousin's violations like the feed of a speed camera. My therapists wanted to talk about shame; I wanted to know about sex. The more curious I got about sex, the more porn I watched. The more porn I watched, the more I wanted to understand the texture of my cousin's perversions. The more I tried to understand his perversions, the faster I developed perversions of my own. The more perversions I explored, the less I understood the limits of desire. Behind the curtain of a sick society, I was off-limits to no one, the shape of my injury a simple search tag in the Redtube database. We are all in common crisis—lending our sex to fantasies (or delusions) of worth.

And as I approached puberty, I could feel the way my short-term glitching was stealing away from a different kind of sight. I watched other girls go unaffected by the terror of growing up in a decontextualized world, watched as the small gears of my body turned against me, executive dysfunction convoluting the word problems that were meant to teach my brain to organize conflict:

[you mouse a cookie if give a]:

math is the same in every language—and cause and effect is too.

"Do you know why you're here?"

The doctor leans down, her hands folded over the chart in her lap. She asks me this, her hair stretched taut at the temples, her whole hairline sitting low on her forehead like a stitch.

Yes, I answer, though I want so badly to give her a cheeky no.

"Because you tried to hurt yourself," she says anyway, as if I didn't know.

I know.

"Okay. Is there something that's been happening that makes you feel this way? At home, at school, anything at all?"

I feel myself growing annoyed already, because obviously. Because I touch a wall and where doesn't it hurt? I know she wants me to give her something she can give to her boss to make them all go home like saviors tonight— a welfare call to Child Services—but I wouldn't give it to them, not this time and never again.

I just get really angry with myself and with other people, which was true and not about my mother.

"What are the things that make you angry?"

I don't know . . . like when people say things about me or threaten me or when I don't get something in class.

"What aren't you getting, and who is threatening you?"

I get everything but math and it makes me so mad. I feel so stupid. I start crying but I can't really explain why, and I don't really want to, to this hospital psych whose job is to evaluate me into an inpatient or outpatient partner facility.

"You're not stupid," she says, and I roll my eyes because what the fuck does she know.

"What else is making you angry?"

I don't know. I can't explain it. I just . . . get really angry at little stuff. It just builds up in me and I feel like I can't control it. Like it's in my throat and I can't breathe unless I scream or hit something.

"Do you hurt other people?" she asks, her voice dropping slightly as if to hide that she's afraid of the answer.

I don't answer her because I don't feel like it. I say, *Sometimes cutting helps, which is why I do that.*

"Yes, you do do that. When you do that, are you trying to kill yourself?"

Not always, I say. Which is true, but is also the only answer if I want to be out of the hospital in under a week.

"You're doing it because you need to be seen then, yeah? I understand that."

Sort of, I say, which is a lie. It was not about being seen at all. I could disappear for all I care. *It's because seeing the blood makes me feel like I'm letting something out. And it helps me stop panicking.*

"Hmm." She puts her clipboard down on her lap and looks out through the small window of the hospital door. "So it's for relief. That makes sense too. The thing is, though—"

And immediately I know where this is about to go. Inside

I start to panic, realizing I shouldn't have said the thing about the blood.

"—you could really hurt yourself, kiddo. And you could wind up doing something you can't undo. And there are people who really care about you! Plus, if you're also hurting other people, that could maybe get you in trouble. We want to make sure you're not hurting yourself or anyone else, right? So here's what I think: I think we should take a couple of days to keep talking and to monitor you while you're here and figure out if there's something we can do long-term to keep you from hurting. Because that's the goal here, huh? To stop you from hurting?"

I was twelve, but this wasn't my first time at the rodeo and I could understand each coded word. She was talking about a two-week stay with a drug course and a possible diagnosis. I looked away but said *sure* to satisfy consent so I could avoid the drama of being strapped to a gurney in the back of an ambulance.

"Good. There's a really great facility with kids just like you across the city with an available bed, but we're going to have to get you there tonight. I'm gonna go talk to your mom."

It's all moving so fast, but it always does. Usually I just get rolled upstairs to the psych ward for a couple days' nap but this time they weren't going to let me go. I can't decide if I want to freak out or go with the flow, but I know I don't want to be detained again, so I begin to snap at the rubber bands on my wrist, hoping the pain will distract me.

My mother comes back in, and I can tell she's relieved. It's been a lot, all too much in fact, and we could all use a breath. Mine would be medicated and I'd grow an appreciation for blue plastic furniture and for losing my sense of time, but fine.

They strap me to the gurney anyway, my warm tears absorbed by the coils at my temples, hands not free enough to dry them.

We get there, my mother leaves, and I remember that my goal is to go home. Like a meditation, I float through the first few days mortified and determined, collecting whatever info I can about what the therapists and doctors needed to hear to believe that I had gotten better and could be let go.

Week one evaded me. I tried, but adjusting to a new drug

requires organizing things about yourself that you thought were innate, having to remind yourself to breathe, to walk when asked to walk, to stand in one swift lift—all things I could not do. In sessions I was quiet and angry. I hated them and I hated this place; it was pathetic and the other kids were pathetic with their weird idiosyncrasies. I was somehow better than the whole thing while a pity to it at the same time, which angered me even more. It humiliated me, I had no privacy, I had no individuality, no autonomy, I wasn't a person, I was a sick kid stuck on the top floor of an armory with some other sick kids and unlike most of them, I knew it.

When the counselor told me I couldn't go home that first Friday, I cried but I wasn't surprised. I focused on getting out.

By Sunday I was a new person and came up with a two-tiered messaging strategy that would focus the conversation on something I didn't care to talk about but could use to emulate growth. I decided that if I could convince them that I understood that my actions were harmful to the people I cared most about, and use my feelings about them to mask my feelings about myself, I could convince the therapist that I was healthy enough for out-patient counseling and could go home. I was drawing pictures of my family, my nonexistent friends, writing letters to my mother—really doing it the fuck up—pretending that I would be good to myself because of how much I loved other people. It was hilarious and also absurd. Of course I loved my mother and my family but how much I loved them wouldn't stop this waning thing in me, its ugliness clawing at my sleep—if love was all it took, I would never have been here but this thing was its own thing, a thing that wanted to kill me, a thing they couldn't fix here, because these doctors didn't understand me, so I was going to have to do it myself.

By Friday I was the star of the institution, my happy smiling face and generous introspection setting an example to other kids for how to charm their way to an extra cookie or an extra juice cup—

> Script: *Even though something really bad happened to me, I know it wasn't my fault, and I know that my self-harm and my fighting is me expressing shame in unhealthy ways, and I know that me being here is how I take that step toward fixing it.*

> :

how to run the game on a system that humiliated you and make it work for you.

My roommate, a precocious bulimic brunette from Queens, shakes her head as I shove my shit in the plastic hospital sack, my last name scribbled on the front in Sharpie. "You're not better at all, are you," she laughs, amazed. "You're worse."

I am, I laugh. *I totally am.*

When my mom comes to get me, we get pizza, and I pray to never go back as I feel the steam from the cheese hit my face, the sun at my ankles joining in holy unison. She asks how I feel as we walk to the subway from the pizza shop, the barbed-wire fence of the top floor of the building I'd just come from hovering above her head like a crown as I look up to answer.

Better, I say, nodding at the thought of having hacked my way out of it all, my two selves coming together to realize a new useful self.

I'm much, much better now.

I discovered: performance allows for ontological sameness. Sameness is believable and qualifying. Sameness is safe.

Every therapist would leave our first session charmed by my introspection, lured by how well adjusted I seemed, *you know, given the circumstances.*

"So, we're glad we did the test, I think it showed us a lot, but unfortunately not quite enough to have a decisive step forward."

"Hmm," my mom hums, waiting for the doctor to elaborate, but based on that hmm I know she already thinks they're about to tell her some bullshit.

"Here's what we know. When she was diagnosed during her stay at Reiss, we found hyperactivity, dissociative behavior, obviously as you know self-destructive behavior—"

I imagine my mom nodding as I hear her hmm again.

"We also documented, based on discussions with school counselors, short tempers and rapid mood swings that escalate quickly—"

"Which explains all the fighting, okay—"

"Right," the psychiatrist says. "So, it could be a number of things, but none we can confirm, simply because she's just too young and there are so many overlapping symptoms. But here's what we've got: it could be ADHD, which would account for the difficulties with coursework—"

"It's just math, though," my mom clarifies, making sure this woman has got the right read, trying to understand—

"Right, that's part of why it's hard to settle there. The way she struggles in that subject doesn't align with her overall skill level. So I have a theory. There's a condition called dyscalculia, which we haven't done a lot of research in and I have yet to diagnose a child with, but is essentially a learning disorder that prevents efficient mathematical comprehension, which could explain the dissociation and daydreaming during class and the careless mistakes, but doesn't necessarily account for the self-harm, the outbursts or the fighting, or the excessive lying."

It's silent for a beat, and I imagine my mom scribbling notes, nodding vigorously.

"Here's what I think: That trauma was an injury. And it changed her chemistry a bit. When you look at all of these symptoms as a composite, there are two conditions that I think of—one called borderline, which is—imagine a rubber band, you stretch and you stretch and you stretch and eventually, once in a while, it snaps.

"The other is bipolar disorder, which, if you imagine, is

a rubber band stretching thin but regularly, with various levels of endurance placed on the band at different times, and sometimes snapping, but often getting so, so thin that the restraint is unreliable.

"Those symptoms of the learning disorder and ADHD are likely symptoms of either one of these disorders, and those symptoms often fall under their umbrella of bipolar disorder, particularly bipolar two.

"The thing is, she's only thirteen, it's much too early to diagnose her for bipolar, but we could begin treating her for borderline if you wanted to pursue that option."

"So which one is it?" my mom asks. "Is it ADHD or borderline?"

"Well, if it's ADHD it's likely borderline, but I don't think it's ADHD, I think it's borderline that shows symptoms as dyscalculia and may later show up as bipo—"

"What's the science behind any of this stuff?" my mom asks, interrupting her.

And it's the last I hear before the vents cut off, and it's nearly silent, the only thing persisting over the sound of the white noise, the murmurs of my mother and this psych.

Soon after, she's storming out, though politely wishing the therapist a "Thank you for all of your help," over her shoulder, letting her know she'll be back in touch soon.

"It's this, it's the other—they just want me to drug up my child. They don't fucking know." I hear my mother suck her perfectly straight, perfectly white teeth, louder than the whistle and screams of the tracks as the 4 train that will take us home shuttles into the station.

She grabs my hand and pulls me near her, with vigor, as we step into a small pooling crowd in front of the subway doors. "My child," she mutters, like a mantra. "You're *my* child. And I will fix you."

She could not fix me. I just got better at it, tried to make being unwell less obvious, less disruptive, for her. For her, for my siblings, their childhoods marred with ERs and perpetual panic—for them, I had to belly this beast of my neural inconsistencies, I had to wrestle it into a harness and bury it down, exorcise it, give it a new dress.

I beat myself into a routine of early functional indepen-
dence and shrugged out of the salt of my sins. All alone
I bare-knuckled my way to self-harm recovery, forcing
myself to stop cutting because it no longer seemed like a
practical medium for relief if I was going to go out into
the world and pass for a girl who was well. Not because
I stopped wanting to. Not because of my pediatrician
threatening that I'd never have a career. It was because
getting older was getting awkward and men were getting
cruel. Because every time I wanted to get naked, I was
sharing the soft parts of my trauma with people I'd never
remember, and I hated the way they'd run the pads of
their fingers over the keloids, kissing at them as if just
then, in the blissful fog of lust, they could heal me. I
couldn't stand the pretense of it all, the role I'd let them
play—me the damsel, them the mare—it made me too
vulnerable, too available, too likely to be exploited.

In the absence of support from literally anyone else, my mother and I became a kind of system, a cross-dependent unit of lateral execution. She would do her best to keep me alive, and I would show up on time to shuttle my sisters home from their after-school classes, to help with homework, to prepare our scant dinners—all this to keep me from boredom, because trouble resumes where boredom resides. But what happened in the brackets of her absence was my business.

As much as I tried to hide, little peeks of it would show up at parent-teacher conferences—teachers mystified by the arrival of a mother whose child had not been seen by school authorities for most of the semester—or a 3:00 A.M. phone call answered groggily to the voice of a man asking if her thirteen-year-old daughter is awake.

At thirteen, I rolled my first spliff, borrowing from the white paper stash beneath my mom's bed, buying nickel bags of seedy dirt from the apartment building's resident dealer.

I get kicked out of school that year for truancy. The next fall, I redo ninth grade in another school. A teacher notes that I seemed to have just *missed* algebra, a guidance counselor notices the cuts on my arms, the pipes of our little secret bursting.

After a little while, with us splitting the housework re-sponsibilities and sparring weekly as our temperaments flared against each other, it came to seem as if there were two women in our house, and not a man anywhere. We became each other's friction, she the belayer, I the rope. I felt a kind of responsibility over the domain. And a per-petual kind of guilt. She should be shielded from the vio-lence of my frayed little mind so that a kind of peace could happen for all of us, allowed to believe that the fixing had worked.

At home, the heat kept rising, my mother's treatment rearing itself ineffective, my disease an attic demon tearing up the floors. I got older and my symptoms got worse. The more I acted out, the angrier she got; the angrier she got, the more I rebelled; and the cycle lends itself to itself. My mom took any sign of disobedience or disorder as evidence that I was punishing her for letting my cousin harm me. The more solipsistic her projections got, the less I felt I needed to hide, since she was going to take up all the space in my illness anyway. The sicker I got, the less patience she had for me. The less patience she had for me, the less grace I reserved for her. The less grace I offered her, the more she seemed to dislike me. The less she seemed to like me, the less of a child I had to be.

This dance consumed us, a dance of whirlwinds where no one else can matter, where we become each other's nightmare, a Freudian complex. We would wax and wane, one day fighting in the kitchen, the next refusing to let go of the other's hand on the way home from school. I would get suspended from school and spend the day trailing behind her like an intern. For half of the day, she was disgusted with me, barely able to feed me lunch—by dinner, we'd be swinging in the porch swing of song, serenading each other on the 12 bus down the Concourse.

Six months after she'd kicked me out for coming out; three weeks after she'd had me arrested and sent to Central Booking during an episode; just a few days after I received my first official, hard-earned paycheck,* I told my mom that I was moving out, this time of my own volition—moving to Brooklyn with Safia, Jamaica, and Kate to get some control over my life. The morning we signed the lease, my mom kicked me out of our Bronx apartment, taking my key in a final exertion of maternal rule. "You want to leave so bad? Fine, leave, and don't come back. I never want to see you here again."

I took it personally, and haven't been back home since.

* You should know, in an earlier draft of this manuscript, I'd neglected to tell you this. In buying this book, you bought rights to your judgment and own it. Your judgment is yours, my mother is mine, and what I don't say in a project about truth is what gets in the way.

At nineteen, I gathered my skirt and went out into the world like this, choosing to leave home with fifty dollars in my pocket, moving two boroughs south to Brooklyn to re-create myself in the glitter of youthful extravagance and the sexy tropes of tortured artistry.

I wanted to be free from the cage of my mind's silent torture, from the violence of my mother's guilty worry, free to print myself out in the world like a watermark, to let my ugliness shimmer in the mirror and my heaviness take swim.

All of my friends were tired, sad, trauma-burdened poets with absent fathers. For one of the first times in my life, I wasn't special, or particularly exceptional, and neither was my clawing, persisting sadness. I fit right in with the other sad, drugged-up girls at the party who couldn't remember the night's conquest but could remember the way he praised her passion, the way he saw her, if only for a mottled moment, for what she really was: a changeling begging to be turned inside out, a Diana who would do anything if he would promise her safety, the protection of dominion.

In the basement of Unnameable Books, white women with merlot-stained and lined lips read prose poems to an audience of the new, the blue, the restless, and me. Many are like diary entries—but I go for the cringe and stay for that rare moment of magic that snicks that pure stretch of skin behind the ear. In the very last row, I wait testily for someone to say something that feels original, or at least familiar. Of course, everyone's Didionian or Plathian, with a modern twist. They're uniquely aware of their white privilege (but that rarely has anything to do with the actual ambition of the poem, it's just some texture for the sake of character development).

Once the poems get past their guilt, the lid lifts, and then we discover that the poem is (actually) about love, or some ordinary heartbreak. It's about the return of a high-school enigma, or a once-ghosted bar hookup who de-scends, gospel-like, into the brunch crowd of a local boutique coffee shop. Out of nowhere, there the love interest appears, aged by the day and bewildered by the main character's wild, cultured beauty, unable to look away. Her flower (a trite and overused but relatively com-mon metaphor for white femme punani) is wet and en-ticed by the memory of their once-taboo attraction, made even wetter by the knowledge that the encounter, however long it might last, would always end in the murk of cold absence—yet, she is compelled to it, she is a disciple.

The choices these poems make are not unique, they are basic, predictable, evergreen, and still of interest to an aging literary canon who are most comfortable with this narrative when it's the white woman writer's domain, and so, for decades, it has been left up to her to lay claim to the femme, the mundane, the cliché, and only she is allowed to make it new, only she can let the rest of us in. But after all this time, even she feels abused by the demands and restrictions of the narrative. What's left of the approach is too singular, too autonomous, and it lacks conviction.

In the dim light of these weekly readings, I can see these seams of struggle, see where the writer's ambitions resist the truth, and see an underdeveloped approach to the function of irony, to two things being true at once, and no approach at all toward the submission it requires to really capture the affects of humiliation. It is, perhaps, too foreign to truly comprehend, unless your life, even in silence, is defined by your resilience to humiliation.

And during a cold year of creative starvation, in which I cannot consider anything beyond my own coruscating agony, it is this and only this that I wish to trade, this burden of context in exchange for the treacle of the cliché. This right here is what I show up for every Wednesday, poems so familiar, so common, so saccharine, they fail me. When I write a love poem, someone calls it proud, tries to mount it, and by then it's lost its use. There is no artful merit in pride. A good love poem's drunk on authority. It's pathetic, self-important, of limited utility, and it fails its audience by design.

In Sanctuary City, the professor with the banging wife and milk-drunk infant sends a vodka Lemon Drop to my seat at the bar and the bartender tucks the man's number into the palm of my hand when I sign my check. My friend wonders why the worst characters in the story are the ones who see me and the ones I choose as subject.

It's magic, I tell her, my magic.

> I'm lying. There's no magic. Just some really backwards fucking math.

Pythagoreans preach that each life adds up to one cumulative journey for your true soul—think of the soul as a string that spans the length of your lifetimes, and that string gets to see a different life every century or so, and each life is a chance, in a series of chances, to build a pathway back to the divine, to wind the string back toward your soul's ultimate home, like traveling the Brick Road to meet Oz.

If you don't like that analogy and God is more your thing, think of it this way: each life is your chance to reconstruct the walkway on your path back to your Creator.

All of this is what Pythagoreans call *successive transmigration,* and according to their gospel, it is only through transmigratory praxis that we make our way back to the fundamentals of true humanity, of a uniting human purpose; it's only through this process that we are able to make sense of the strange chemistry that makes the eye see green.

It is through living, then dying, and living to die again that we discover what being alive is supposed to mean at all.

On the roof of my thirty-floor high-rise, I smoke what I have decided, in my manic state, is my last cigarette. My cellphone vibrates with one call after another. After a couple shaky sips of nicotine, I answer. It's *M*. "I'm almost there. I'm almost there. I'm almost there."

Part II
TO SQUARE

To make this worth your time, there are a couple of things I'm going to have to do that I really don't want to do for the integrity of your experience:

1) Make sure you know that *I* know how much of the corrosion was his. I'm not protecting him from your perceptions, or misremembering his failures, but now that I've got my wits about me, I'd like to be efficient and I don't have time to tell you his whole story *and* mine. Call it a repair economy.

2) I'll have to tell you about what felt good, what his face did to my blood when I saw him first, and how we got this way.

Through most of my late teens and early twenties, I'd been convinced that songwriting and singing was my calling, or at least part of it. Working alone wasn't working anymore; I needed a partner. A friend connected us— X thought I had a good voice and could write. I was just glad he had a drum machine. The agreement was simple: he was to be my producer. He'd make the beats and I'd write the love song in the key of his choice, give it the scale our dreams deserved.

Early on, he nicknamed me Holyfield, a name I tack to the vision board of who I think I might be in any honest version of myself. When I forget, even now, he slips it into my pocket, a portkey.

That first night we met, at the suggestion of a mutual friend, X and I planned to link up at what was then my favorite neighborhood bar, opting to sit opposite each other, our knees shoved unnaturally into the belly compartment of a Pac-Man console refurbished as a table, the view of the snowy exterior hot like steam. When he walked in and sat down across from me, that smile stretching slow across his cheeks like molasses, I could feel something glowing in the hidden-most part of my chest, a glow that made my heart sick with shine, gripped me by my collarbone, and the whole time I leaned forward, like an arrow in its quiver.

After talking for three hours, we finally venture out of the bar, the rain so heavy it hurts, the universe squeezing us into that small pod of dry space beneath the shelter of my umbrella, where his breath makes shapes in my breath as we walk the six long Bed-Stuy blocks to my apartment, his shoulder respectfully grazing mine. I ask him: *Do you want to get high with me?* X says yes, like he's in a trance. It's the end of the night, and I know him now.

Upstairs, I pack a bowl of the brick weed I travel an hour and a half uptown to buy. Gently, as if afraid to offend me, he remarks on its purple-black darkness and density. I tell him the weed is bruised, like me. He fidgets as he attempts to adjust in the seat of the desk chair in the corner of my bedroom, folding one leg over a knee, then again with the other. In this shoebox of a space, X is four feet away from the foot of my bed but so, so close to me I could smell the work on him. He sits there, unnaturally still except to pass the bowl back to me every few moments, his eyes hanging on to every one of my words, his tender laughter strumming the quiet tension like fingers on a harp.

Born in Philly, raised in South Jersey, Pisces Sun, Pisces Moon, born to a gaggle of tiny witches, born in the dead of March, the roads white from winter wear. Turned ten in the year of Columbine, no longer believes in God (but please, no one tell his nana about that), smokes Marlboro 27s, the pack that almost looks like real gold. Truck driver for a garbage disposal company, a music degree from a small college in a small college town that he will never use for anything more than blistered nostalgia. A knack for jumping from one pot to the other when the heat goes stale.

What I loved about his music was its familiar melancho-
lia, its darkness soft and complex, like summer's retreat.
Something ugly was haunting him too. It was so much
like the music I wanted to make—sad-scared-girl-
mumble-RnB—and here I had found the illusory maestro of my dreams. He saw that rivulet of need whistling
through me, put his mouth to it, and I became his Eve.

The first time X kissed me, it felt like I'd been reborn into a world I'd been banished from, a fractured heart being my means of excommunication, a full one willing me back. It's the way the stupefying glare of his ambient mood lights touched the tip of his nose, or how he looked at me in the almost-darkness, like he was scoring every single emotion. It's the way my mask fell like a cloth released. It's like he knew there was something inside of me that was at the end. It's the way he immediately held my hand with not a single bead of trepidation, like he knew I was his, like he knew he had to walk beside me to get ahead of himself. It's the way he could have been afraid, and was, but came for me, came to get me, would not let me ignore him, would not let me see past him. It's the way his generosity became his only currency, spending every dollar of it on my needs and needing so little in return. It's the way I knew that all I had to do was love him back to deserve how much he loved me. It's the way the darkest parts of my self quivered as his love approached me, the seams of what separates me suddenly loose. I wasn't sure, but I had ambition.

One night, after he played a new beat for me and smoked me out, our faces were suddenly inches from each other. I expected the kiss but didn't expect to be so gripped by it, restrained by the symmetry and strength of his lips, unable to pull apart.

Just days later, he was baking a cake for my birthday, had bought me the new Nicki Minaj album, and a couple twenties' worth of Victoria's Secret panties. My flight-or-fight triggered, my two selves unsure of how to step into the ease of this new ontological conflict, of how to manage my nature and learn to give what I felt so inspired to receive. I freaked out, disappearing for six weeks, popping up once in a blue moon with cautious, open-ended texts to hem the silence, to make sure he was still there.

We were broke and working service jobs that paid us more than we'd ever made. We were young and pregnant with unfair dreams. One wanted to tour the world and shift the soundscape—the other wanted the same. At first it seemed like sickle and sun; Leopold and Loeb—desires of different origins; complementary but one. We were fighting for the other's sense of significance, giving everything we could to the other's confidence. I loved his approach to sound-making and he loved to hear me sing.

My mom told me that my grandma told her that we were cursed. She said that one of us, in a past life, had killed a priest or stolen from a god, and thus, our love lives would be marked with cruelty, abandon, and martyrdom. I can't imagine how we'd ever be important enough to justice's arc as to elicit such pointed karmic revenge, but what the fuck do I know. I found it a fantastic and self-indulgent lie and I wasn't surprised that my mother believed it; it was good drama, but it wouldn't be mine.

Haunted by the threat of perpetual incompletion, I wanted to be able to say I did a hard thing well without being pulled to the cross about it, that I learned to bury the worst of myself for someone else's happiness, the sharp remains of my unresolved youth-hood clinging to the underbelly of my ambition, begging to be taken with. He, so selflessly, wanted to love me, all of me, would take me with my volume, would take me from my victim-hood, would give me a lease on a different kind of life.

So I killed the character of indecision, took him to dinner for his birthday, got tipsy in his backyard, and told him I loved him back, the rain nipping at my nose like a whistle.

Before him there was *J*.

J was Italian white and very cute and very smart and very kinky and very intense. I remember thinking that I could never love anyone more than I loved him. I was (obviously) incorrect.

J was creamy and olivey and blue eyed and Aryan and wanted me, which, based on my juvenile, colonized-ass logic, made me superior, even to myself, even if just momentarily, even if I only bloomed under the green lye of his masochistic study. At nineteen, I could have wanted for nothing more pure than this—a juvenile love cultivated by the very fact of my new adult autonomy and my contradicting need to be owned.

So when *J* graduated from college and got his first real adult job, we moved into a small basement apartment in Connecticut, completely isolated from anyone I'd ever known and would ever know, sometimes missing out on sunlight for days.

I just knew this was love: domestic instincts activated, my chicken salads with various stone fruits as the feature, my laundry and vacuuming, the ugliest parts of my personality muted by my desperation, my need winning out, my crying and wall-climbing, my ravenous desire to feel the sun on my face, my skin graying from a lack of vitamin D—I just knew it. And who could tell me any different? Who could tell me that what I'd come to learn in the living room of this love was only a combat course, a rookie's introduction to the interface?

And then I met X and needed him more than I had ever needed anyone in my life, which was not something I could mask, which was dire and damning and desperate. I was vulnerable in a way I had not known, and once vulnerable, I was less capable of playing the versions of myself that I had learned to play to get through. Under his love, I was a werewolf at the turn of the moon, and I let the sun in me set to it.

Maybe five months into being officially together, I find myself trapped in the eye of an awful, debilitating spiral.

Long before whatever triggered me had triggered me, X had made plans to get coffee with his most recent ex-girlfriend. It was devastating, the idea of him being gone for two-plus hours with a woman whom he had once loved, who was not the woman weeping mercilessly in his bed about nothing. Something about our closeness had triggered an abandonment complex I didn't even realize I'd had and I couldn't process the thought of him leaving me. That was the first day he saw it too, how wounding and lethal I could be to myself, and how it was not normal. I could see the panic in his eyes—that helpless desire to help me, to rescue his true love, that helpless desire to escape. He leaves. He returns. I am in the same spot he had left me in. He walks in and leans over me to open the shades and let the dusklight in, then he wraps me in his wingspan, folding me into him, as if he has been thinking about doing this for hours. I lean into his embrace and cry even harder as he pulls me tighter. *I'm sorry I'm like this,* I tell him, *I don't know why I'm like this.*

"It's okay," he coos into my hair, his hand fastened to the back of my neck. "It's okay. You can be like this. You don't have to be anything else."

People are systems. Systems are motivated and organized by mathematical impulses: To stay? Or to go? To run? Or to hide? To bite? Or to scratch? We know what punctures allow for blood. We know the vulnerable bricks. We know where to pull a thread if we want to tender an unraveling.

It wasn't always what it became. We weren't. I don't think. I spent much of it swaddled in the warm womb of his golden admiration, *X*'s eyes bloated with the blood of me, his hands bound. For the first time, I was no one's taboo, I was actually perfect and preferred and common-place, just a girl who was just right for a man deep in his own transposition.

[fields of roses. All different kinds.]

His favorite aunt has the pain threshold of your dreams. She's the smartest one in the family, afraid of nothing but her own ambition, has been chain-smoking for years. When we first met, she was pleasant but distant and studied me from the corner of the blond-lit kitchen, waiting for any opportunity to wave the red flag. I was impressed, humbled for X—how incredible to be loved so carefully, to be a grown man still swaddled by the warmth of others' cautions.

Near the pool, she told me how special she thought I was. She told me if I hurt her nephew, she'd know exactly where to find me.

One summer, he'd gone through a calendar and made little notes, set tiny dates—a walking tour here, Pokémon Go trip there—cute, considerate, perfect of him.

[caressing *X*'s face in the dawn of 4:00 A.M. as we trip through the flat spiral of a psychedelic high, my mouth dry with dappled desire, his body thick with fancy.]

One day, on the earlier end of our relationship, my friends asked if I ever thought he'd cheat on me. I laughed from the seed of my belly, slapping the table and everything.

What? No, of course not. Me? He's obsessed with me.

We all chuckled with smug exactitude, precise and final.

Of course not.

Me?

[his curious little cousin watching us kiss at Christmas, the flutter of her lashes as she asks us when we're getting married.]

[the numbing taste of cocaine on my lips as we stare into the long hallways of each other's eyes, the world of the Lower East Side bar absent to us, *only this one, only this.*]

[the bell of his laughter whistling through the house. His
ziti; his ziti; his ziti.]

[the shared Pinterest pages, pins of wedding bliss to in-
spire our own.]

[his offering on my returns home—blunt in the ashtray, fresh-baked cookies on the counter, flowers in their vase.]

But it's these polyps of memory that make it hard to trust the stuff of certainty:

Six months into our new living situation, a little over a year into our relationship, the honeymoon bliss like wax on the walls, I notice he's less interested in making things with me, less interested in letting me in on his studio time. I ask him for a beat to write to and he denies me. I interrogate this subtly, writing alone then asking him to review, to help me solidify a melody. He's not into it and I'm confused. I'd been growing lyrically, he'd been growing musically, we'd been growing toward each other, but now we seemed to be growing apart.

One insufferable night, I give up the subtle approach, ask him outright why he won't make shit with me. As if struck with the lightning of an irritation he can't mask, he turns to me sharply and asks me a series of questions:

"Do you love music?"

"What do you love more—this, poetry, or politics?"

I would choose writing over anything, he knows this.

He calls my silence a confirmation.

"This"—he says as he points to the dashboard of drums—
"is the only thing I am good at. And I don't want to
compete with you to be good at it. It's mine. I don't want
to share it with you."

The entire premise of our relationship goes up in a smoke of purist hubris.

That conversation was disorienting, but brought an orientation to our bits, made me know what was his place and what was mine. The stillness, the passive negotiating. Days went by; I felt less like a lover and more like a wife. I thought I liked it. Could get used to it.

And then I got bored.

Do I dare?   *Do I dare?*

Where to put this blinding focus, this fire of dreams? When I'm like this, all I know is my compulsive desire to be inside out, to be the limit, to barely but finally exist. Of what I don't have, suddenly I am in desperate need. What cannot satiate me becomes speed.

A factorial is, in essence, a summation. Here is what you get when you add up all the early derivatives, when you collect mass in sequence, when $1 + 1 = 2$, and $2 + 1$ condenses to become 3. This arithmetic is the orchestral hum of humanity, the illustration of exponential growth.

Always in your body there is a need unmet.

They were always people he would never meet. I made fake profiles on dating apps and sugar sites just to browse, to flirt, to share meaningless perversions with people whose perversions would never leave the internet, not long enough to ever meet me. But whatever satisfaction I gleaned soon wore off. Chasing it, I moved on to flirting with childhood friends two boroughs away who would never come to Brooklyn; I hooked up with ex-girlfriends he wouldn't suspect if they did meet him; with my seatmate on the way to London; with my workshop mate in London; with the courier in Florence; with the store manager in Florence; the chef in Florence; with the basketball player in Wisconsin; the graduate student in Cambridge; the bartender in Waco; the venue hosts at Nationals; the venue hosts at the slam in Atlanta; that one poet I fell in love with that one summer in Pittsburgh, his lips swollen from the vigor of our need, saying to me over and over again, "You're exactly the kind of girl I want to need."

When I got home from Pittsburgh, I was a fucking wreck.

I had been crying for five hours over the unjust loss of a brand-new love, like a tween riding home alone on the bus from camp. I had known him for approximately five days. I didn't even notice him until three days into the retreat—three days into three-hour nights of sleep, five-hour days of drinking, many hours of crying when I felt that violent ache of my own yearning. It hovered in me, taking up new space. I was vibrating with it. I needed to be seen, touched, adored, like an ornament. His attention gave me something to focus on, a channel to reprogram the trajectory of my spiral. We fell into some kind of suspended, manic dream, the edges of my view crisp with delusion as we told each other tales of how perfect we would be for each other in real life.

On the last night of the retreat, I could feel the humiliation tiptoeing around the corner, coming toward me, positioned to yoke me, as he played hot and cold through the night, until finally he admitted that he'd thought about it some more and really couldn't make room for me, not with his two girlfriends already expecting the rest of himself. A friendly deer, backlit by the prism of purple, approached me slow and let me touch its cheek. I drank and drank and drank until the night sat down and the sun became a menace. I ended up weeping in his arms at his rejection well into the morning light, absolutely bleeding from it, him rocking me in his lap and apologizing for not having space for me.

I got home later that morning and leapt into X's arms like I'd been taken from him, like I'd been lost. I cried and he begged to know what was wrong—"What is it? What happened? Baby, what's wrong?"

[the drunken half-mile walk to the good taco truck on
Thirty-first Street at midnight.]

When I asked for an open relationship, really, there were many logics at play.

Love itself is an unfair bargain and most of the time it's missing the point.

Who would I be if not a woman who can run up against the tides of her clichés?

I had already cheated.

We had long before stopped being able to fulfill each other and I thought external reassurance might light a match.

I could feel his growing resentment scathing me, could feel it stifling him, closing in on his creative channels—we lived together, all he saw was me, I thought he needed some diversity, an intermission. I thought some mischief, a little diversity of impact could wake something up in us, get us back to the place where our fires burned together.

And I just wanted to stop lying.

When I brought it up he said, "Yes, I would like to try," and as he says it, I can see the iris of his eye flicker gold with doubt.

A fractal is a never-ending pattern, infinitely complex. It reproduces itself in perpetuity, in everything, hiding around and inside of us, like Russian dolls, like a forest bordered by and stuffed full with sisters of trees. A river that splits and meets itself in the mouth of another river. A simple equation processed over and over again, like a stamp, like your DNA, like your brain, like your lungs, like a mother.

I've been curious lately about how the self reproduces itself within itself, its patterns permuting and duplicating in foreign systems, like fractals do, like the Mandelbrot set, never ending, the fingerprint of God.

He's too needy, I tell Netta, and I'm not being coy or hyperbolic, I'm more serious than I'd like to be. When I'm honest with myself I know that the last thing I need is to be is needed, at least in the way he needs to be needed. Keeping up this performance had exhausted me, gotten old. I don't want to carry it or have to water it. I don't want to have to forage nor would I like to feed it, not because I don't value it but because I can't remember it, because I forget my keys, because I forget to eat, because I forget that humanness is a thing that has to be tilled and cultivated. I'm going through the world real nimble, just vibes, like a hum, and *X* and I are so beautiful, so precious, so ginger, and consciously I fear that he will break me but subconsciously I know that I will break the fourth wall and be what breaks us both.

Betty Draper is giving birth, and it isn't going well. She falls into a fever dream (or a garden psychosis), and the intercom whispers, *The doctor will be here and there.* In her dream, a puppeted caterpillar falls into her palm, its neck on crane. She wants to escape, the end of this hell is just there, but her father appears from his place in the death-scape to tell her what she already knows: *You're a house cat. You're very important, and you have little to do.*

Six months into my first real political job, I fell into the worst cycle I'd had since X and I had gotten together, my irritability like the landing bed of a match. I had developed rosacea all over my body from the stress of the job and the stress of full-time grad school and the stress of my illness (the stress of hiding my illness).

And then it was the third month in a row where X couldn't pay his half of the rent, and this month, even though I knew it was relatively out of his control, it felt like a violence, like something he had done to me to punish me for choosing him.

On the other end of the phone, my mom attempts to weather my panicky babbling as I yell at the top of my lungs, my mania impenetrable. She yells over me, the familiar lilt of her Caribbean accent shocking me into silence, "Leave him then! If being with him is making you spiral like this, then be alone!"

I can't leave him, I tell her, this is the trap I set myself up in, it was him or nothing, this was it. My mother, exasperated, says, "Well, if you think you're stuck, then you're stuck."

Just then, he enters our apartment, his face a peculiar red shade of summer brown. "I heard you," he says, walking by me, refusing to look at my face. "I heard what you said. And your mom is right."

He walks into our spare bedroom, closes the door, and locks it. I only know this in retrospect, but that night, they both gave me permission to stop performing.

I can feel the difference between being in and out of the know like an itch on my arm. Where before, we'd traveled through the darkness of Brooklyn like wayward twins, weaved and wedded in need, now we were like two wives, one left at home until dawn while the other went out to explore the dirty trails of their own worlds alone.

He was walking into our apartment at 4:00 A.M., wasted, his shadow trembling from twelve hours of drinking. Terrified (of the obvious—the police; the subway tracks; his drunk temper and the street), I would wake up at 3:00 A.M. searching for him, and he would walk in just as I was about to doze off again, whispering to me that he'd come from an after-party (*on a Tuesday, my G?*) and needed to shower. Then he'd crawl into bed for the ten minutes between his bedtime and my rising, clutching at my body like it was a secret. And something wasn't right but at the same time, not a lot was wrong.

After all, this is what I wanted for him, the kind of freedom that would make him the main character in his own life so that I could live a kind of freedom where my desires were most important—but I had an inkling that he was lying and there was something about it that had sparked a brush in the corner of the barn.

Every day I grew more skeptical and every day I grew more desperate, his texts becoming more sparse, our date nights like funerals. And what the fuck was he so sad about? I thought it was his other shit, his own shit, but his resentment seemed so acute, orchestrated, earmarked for me. Where, just months before, he'd texted me at two in the morning about how badly he wanted to be home with me, inside of me, "instead of at this bar," with "these people," we were going whole days with no exchange, with no "home soon," with no "wait up for me." There was something going on and I could see it bulging out of his pockets when he walked through the door.

I'm buying lingerie and finding them one size too small. I'm planning dinners he's not showing up for. When he is home, he's telling me short stories about his time at these after-parties, the parties themselves deceptively un-eventful, the narrative gaps gaping, the names literally unbelievable. How do you know when the love of your life is lying to you? Every smile is forlorn. He's so sorry for something he can't ever articulate. You watch a rom-com, and he's nostalgic. When he has so little to say. When nothing he says satisfies. When the inch-sized si-lence becomes a delta.

But he's adding pins to the wedding Pinterest . . . he's reconciling potential wedding dates with other future planning (at no special request from me) . . . he's signing spontaneous Instagram posts about me with "until the end of time" . . . his friends and family are heart-heart-hearting in the comments . . .

On the other side of the freeway, traffic stalls to better observe the three-car pileup clogging the middle of the road. We slow down to get as close a glimpse as we can at the mangled metal, the twisted roofs punctuating each other with their new angles, with their sharp lines. From where we sit, a mere twenty feet away, our heads craning low out of the windows, it is still impossible to know who holds ultimate fault in this tragedy, who to send the bill to. All the cars are the same color, the same size, the same make, 1997 white Acuras—in the end, the fault could belong to any one of them: the one distracted by her girlfriend's rage text on the way home; the one playfully racing with the station wagon in the lane next to him; the one jerking off behind the wheel. Any one of them could be the fatal other, the one with the confession to make upon meeting their maker, but regardless, in the end, even the one least responsible for the final output at least had the choice of the input in hand. From over here, all of the victims are villains, and all of the villains are dead.

It was when the girl he was messing with said, "It's just a breakup—you'll both get over this," that I started to get a little pissed off.

First of all,

I was already willing to make some simple compromises—
if she wanted him at 4:00 A.M., she could have him. I
entered the group chat thinking that our feminisms would
take precedence over his underwhelming lies.

But since she was so interested in my anguish, I was happy to share with her our secrets of callous betrayal, to let her in on our toxic matrix.

No, YOU don't get it, I tell her over Facebook Messenger, the new interface perfectly blinding and white, *I just had an abortion four months ago. He doesn't really love you, he's just really fucking angry at me.*

I'll never forget what it felt like to be pregnant. To feel like a host body. To feel something needful flourish inside of you, feeding on the little you have to give. To feel what it's like to be divided in real time. Separating what you've sewn up. I'll never forget how I felt that one morning when I knew, not sick but full, too full though I had not eaten, how I would touch my lower belly and feel steel. I will never forget the urgency of the question, how it tore up my day, how it was the only thing I could think about. I'll never forget how I just *knew*, I knew it before confirmation, and how quickly I calculated the cost, the analysis speeding ahead of me. I'll never forget my resolve, how patiently I waited for the nurse on the other end of the phone to confirm my appointment, how I said, *Yes, I'll find the money*, though I had none and no clue where we would get it. I'll never forget what it felt like to carry both our futures in the purse of my humanness, the difference only a twenty-minute procedure, how I thought he would be so proud of me for saving him from a lifetime of inevitable, insurmountable impossibilities.

It was when we were in the first throes of breaking up that he grieved it for the first time. "You took my chance," he yelled, throwing a glass across the room, it shattering against the brick wall, "you took my chance at being a father and you didn't even fucking ask me what I wanted. You didn't even fucking ask."

I didn't know. I swear, I didn't know. If I knew, I would have kept it, but you didn't say anything.

"You didn't even fucking ask."

Everything is starting to fall apart—I'm making stupid, irresponsible mistakes at work—my irritability is peaking at odd intervals—I'm fucking up formulas and misjudging outputs.

At the urgent care, while being treated for a severe kidney infection born from an untreated UTI I didn't even know I'd had, the doctor asks, "Sweetheart, you didn't feel any of the symptoms?"

No, I said. *Not until today.*

I leave our apartment for a few days, hoping that time apart will help him make better choices and help me feel less alone. During that three-day stay away, crashing at a friend's Airbnb, I had convinced myself that this would be our redemption story, that we would come back from this like champions, phoenixes rising from the ashes of our own bitter bullshit. No one who loves me shared this optimism.

Collective concern grows, and after many unanswered door knocks and rejected phone calls, I crawl out of my grotto, follow my feet mindlessly, and I end up in Bed–Stuy, on Grand, at *M*'s place, to drink wine, smoke weed, read tarot, and forget my own name.

After I've had a glass, the shell of my shield starts to crack and before I know it I'm crying in the cup of my hands, the water overflowing. *I'm not okay, I don't think,* I say with emphasis on okay, just to make it clear, and *M* chuckles, "Uh, yeah girl, you're definitely not okay.

"Because this is really bad, and if I were you, I would be in a puddle, in the corner, also crying my fucking eyes out."

It feels like for the first time someone has admitted that this was a particularly unique and traumatic situation and that my angst was not purely dramatized but fairly earned and accurate. They would want to die too, right? *You would, right?* I ask, my hands flinging out ahead of me with a broken exasperation, and *A* says, "Yes, of course, we all would," and for a second, I let them be right, knowing they're probably wrong.

My friends could only offer their practiced condolences, "You were too good for him," or "He didn't deserve you." No one let me say it, because everyone wanted me to be strong. No one let me say it—I let my walls down and I miscalculated my shot, misunderstood the assignment, and in the end I hurt myself. I really hurt myself, and I felt too guilty to ask permission for it to be my fault.

But when I was alone, I could say it to the bottom of the vodka bottle. I could get wasted and relapse and listen to music that made me cry and daydream about the different ways I wanted to be remembered.

Existence is a temporal trap, a 360 trip wire, our past and future selves meeting each other for the first time every day of our lives.

"Have you looked into going to see someone?"

My last therapist quit, I whisper after a beat to my best friend, my head pounding against the cold wall of the bathroom stall after heaving my insides into the proverbial basin of significant regret.

"What? You didn't tell me that. Why?"

Yeah, the second one this year. Said she wasn't equipped to counsel me because of my history with suicide and self-harm and shit—

"I'm sorry, isn't that the job of a therapist?"

I don't say anything because I've already traveled this thought pattern and had the same questions and had come to no resolve.

"We have to get you a new one, dude."

It's too stressful, I whisper. They gave me some referrals but I can't keep telling people my life story over and over again for them to tell me it's too complicated and that they can't help me.

I just need to get over this, like anyone-fucking-else who goes through a breakup.

"But you're not just going through a breakup, C. You know that."

It's my mother who first introduced me to Shakespeare.

BANQUO

Were such things here as we do speak about,
Or have we eaten on the insane root
That takes the reason prisoner?

In *The Life of Pythagoras* or *On the Pythagorean Life,* Iamblichus writes that death is a migration, and that the life you lived before death is what trains you to resist the descent into the lower levels of existence.

I don't know what those lower levels are, but I can guarantee that I have felt pulled to them. Constantly attending to descent in the hard work of anamnesis.

Pythagoreans believed that there are three ways humanity improves, one of which is dying. Death is biological, but where it is also metaphysical is where I find delight.

Moving day felt nothing like the day I left my mother's home, or any other day where I leave a thing behind that had inhabited me. But I had done well with what will I'd had. I'd woken up, and look, the sun even came out to show its diffident smile. I had packed my things efficiently, hummingly evading anything that would remind me of him, or me.

In my new bedroom, I order comfort food from Seamless, a good bottle of tequila on FreshDirect. My father stops by, and I say, *Shit happens, it'll be fine.* I had not called X one time, I had gone through the entire day not needing him, not needing him to need me to need him, completely independent from the quiet nightmare nipping at my heels.

Late that same night, I'm nearly inside out with the blue light of grief. I feel like I've been blown through, some invisible glow casting my shadow on the wall. I can't think, I can't see, I can't breathe. I press the blade to the innermost part of my thigh, where I know the blood will babble if released, and tug the thick blade across my thigh, the sharp stain of the knife on my nerves dissipating almost instantly. It's not enough. I press the blade to a patch of skin just above it, and tug. I can breathe again, but it's not enough. Finally, at the fifth tug, the crimson drops begin to gather into one big metadrop, the babble finding its stream. When I started to cut I learned that the first cut is never enough because your body forgets what it feels like and you need it to remember. I go and go and go until there's no thigh left unmarked.

Math is a form of faith, a faith of its own dynamic and complex language system, and to speak it is to agree to its principles: Input begets output. One becomes the other. One variable is subject to the mechanics of the others. You give what you get. You get what you are prepared to receive.

[the wedding date we set, its incident come and gone like waxwings in the deep south of winter.]

In the first days after we separate, it's the sleeplessness that bonds us. Over the phone, we cling to the rhythms of each other's breath to help calibrate our own. I'm falling asleep, but I want him to make it known: I'm not the only one limbless in the small sac of despair. He'll never say it, though, and he'll never let me go. He wants to know that I'll be dedicated enough to await his permission or dismissal. His revenge happens in the thrill of knowing that I'm there. We are twins; his entire praxis is a wounded manhood. I treat his cut with my own murder. I swell it up to size.

[*X*'s grandmother holding my cheeks, her crooked tooth
a diamond in the pillows of her mouth.]

Everyone goes through a breakup. Every single one of us. Every one of us finds romance and loses it, sometimes in the same breath, sometimes in a lifetime, how come I was the one who couldn't endure?

This was no suffrage. My mother said, "It just is what it is," and it felt rudely simple of a gesture but in the grand scheme of things, she couldn't be wrong. It is, and it was, what it was—and there was not a death that would undo it. But it did not feel that simple inside. It did not feel like a six-syllable soliloquy, it felt like a six-syllable sentence, a prison of perpetual abandonment, someone leaving me raw and open every day, like Icarus.

I kept saying—to her, to my friends, to anyone who would listen—*I feel like I am going to die,* and it was like no one heard what I said. I kept saying it, how my heart is on fire and I don't think I can breathe.

My rage had taken over. My heart engulfed in the clay of heat, I was going to die. The only person I didn't have to convince was *M.* I text a hurried warning, and she calls in an instant:

"Hold on. Just stay right there. Give me five minutes and I'll be right there. Let's distract you while you wait. Can you pack a bag? We gotta take you in."

Part III

THE FINAL VALUE

As it turns out nature has a formula that tells us when it's an entity's time to die.

A death brings you back to life; washes you in the blood; sanctifies you.

When I come home from the hospital this time, it's like it always is but it is also very different. My friends from grad school come to pick me up and going home is not like going home. No mother to prove wellness to, to try for, pirouetting to the tip-tap of my solitary weeping, just me and my strange need dancing in the mirror of my strange need.

I called out of work, told my boss that I was sick, achy, didn't tell her with what—really, what was there to say? What I needed was sleep, not pity. When I got into the office the next day, I decided to be honest, tell her I was going through an earth-shattering transition and was not going to be well. With empathy as real as a Hallmark Basquiat, she encouraged me to throw myself into work as a distraction, reminding me that pain is tentative and will pass if you ignore it.

The late R train to Cortlandt Street becomes my safest haven. I'm crying into my coat on the way to work, reapplying concealer in the bathroom stall before walking into our morning meeting, where the rest of my team turns to me expectantly for updates, of which I have significantly fewer than I should. The next day, I send out a press release with four typos. Later in the week, I confuse one client's crisis for another's. The next week, I respond to an email marked urgent that I left unread for five days. On an unbearable random Thursday at lunchtime, I call it a day, take the gamble and leave early, buy a bottle of prosecco, and walk down to the South Street Seaport pier. The sun is out and I'm out of crosses.

The outpatient psychiatrist's office is suffocatingly tight. Many of the patients treated here are suffering from addiction and are either fresh out of an incarceration facility or on the brink of being sent to one, this pit stop at the doc's the only difference between being here or being there. You can feel the formal intensity of that constant truth buzzing with the lights, hanging at eye level in the room.

"So, I see here you have a history of self-harm," he begins.

I nod yes.

"Is that still going on?" he asks.

Sometimes, but not as much as before.

"How much is not as much as before, like once a week, once a month . . . ?" he prods.

Like once every four or five months, maybe more.

"And when does that happen?" he asks, which I've got to tell you, I'm sick of answering at this point in my life.

When I'm upset. If I feel overly frustrated, it kind of blurs my vision, makes things really crisp at the edges. I can't see and I'm just really pissed off and out of it. That's when.

"I see it says you have ADHD? Can I see your test?"

I reach for my phone and pull up the charts I'd gotten from an ADHD and learning disorder screening test a couple of months before, nervous that the doctor would find some inconsistency and say the test was fake or invalid.

"I am familiar with this test center, good. Wow. Interesting."

I cock my head to the side to look beside him, curious to know what he's seeing that I hadn't.

"There must be something else going on here. Just being honest," he says, as if asking my permission to offend me. "If you only had ADHD, you wouldn't have gotten past the fourth grade without real treatment, and you're clearly successful. You could be a miracle, but I doubt it."

Stunned by his candidness, I laugh—*yeah, probably not a miracle.*

"Do you do drugs?" he asks.

What kind of drugs? I lob back.

"Stimulants," he asks; he squints. "Coke."

I have, I say, averting my eyes but only for a moment, to not allow shame in the room.

"And how does it make you feel?" he asks.

Honestly? Weirdly enough, it usually makes me sleepy.

"And do you actually fall asleep?" he asks.

Sometimes.

"Hmm. I ask because this is typical of people with bipolar two; don't worry, I'm not a cop."

Ha, I laugh, *good to know you're not a cop.*

I answer more of his questions, and finally he asks, "Do you think there's a possibility that you're bipolar based on what I've told you and what you've told me?"

I think so? When I was younger I think I remember one doctor mentioning it, but then never again, so I thought it could just be regular depression, or an anger issue or—

"You're bipolar," he says, interrupting me. "You have bipolar two. It often gets confused with ADHD because there are shared symptoms, but yours is marked by periods of high productivity and low lows. It's part of why you've had so many suicide attempts but seem to bounce back," he says with air quotes. "You're high-performing but your shorter spurts of manic or depressive episodes are marked by extreme mood swings. It's very dangerous. It's quite lucky you're alive."

I mean, I think so, I say.

"Yes," he says. "You should."

It's bipolar, I tell my mom, yelling over sirens as I shift nervously from foot to foot while standing on the busy corner of Smith and Livingston, thirty-three flights below her office, where she shuffles legal-sized pages across her desk in the hurry of a busy workday.

I'm bipolar, I say, more quietly this time as the sirens pull away.

"That makes sense. They kind of told me that would happen," she says, matter-of-factly, like it wasn't something I might have wanted to know. I tell her that.

"It wasn't. You had it bad enough, no need to tell you that you would essentially suffer forever."

We're silent for a beat—me trying to understand the tail of that sentence, her contending with the fact that she had said it.

I'm not going to suffer forever, I say quietly, like there's an amplifier in my throat.

"I didn't mean it that way," she says. "I just didn't want you to think of it that way then.

"Well, anyway, now you know."

Yeah. They gave me meds, I say, shifting my weight again and looking over my shoulder, half sure she can see me. *You know I hate meds.*

"That's because they made you zonked out when you were a kid. You told me you didn't want them anymore, so I stopped it. You're grown now, though, so advocate for yourself. If it's not working, tell somebody, don't let them drug you up if it won't help."

How do I know, though? If it's working?

My mom sighs like I'm behind in this conversation and she's been ready to move on. "I don't know, babe, you gotta ask the doctors."

It had been hers for so long, this burden. Masking was me thinking the labor of hiding was equivalent to the labor of care, but it was a convenient lie we both let me tell.

And so here we are, filling a prescription for a stabilizer at the Duane Reade on the corner of Jay and MetroTech. I'm tapping my foot and looking at the pharmacist and assistants from under my shades, sweating, wondering if they can know what the medicines I'm picking up mean about me. I also remember that one of the drugs is a drug often prescribed to people who suffer from seizures, so maybe none of this meant anything at all.

> Day one was a colorful day; everything moved much faster and my body felt much warmer, the sun somehow following my lead.
>
> Day two was up and down, as if my hormones were on an axis, dipping in and out of my cerebellum at various levels, much too much, and much too little all at once.
>
> Day three was like day two.
>
> Day four was like day two.
>
> Day five was like day three, which was slightly better than day two but still generally trash.

I forgot what it felt like after day six. I also forgot to eat. For the first time in a long time, I realized that I could hear one voice talking in my head instead of five voices, interrupting each other, contradicting each other. I felt like a reverb: slow, consistent, where finally I could feel myself making sense, and I could feel nothing else.

In the immediate aftermath of my diagnosis, I spend the odd hours of the morning searching the deepest caverns of the internet for ways to understand my sickness. I was obsessed with it, a fantastical discovery, a tiny key to a series of locks I'd never even noticed. I couldn't stop texting my friends with new things I'd learned about the disease, and about myself.

On a casual lunchtime walk with my mom in the spring, as we cross Flatbush Avenue Extension, I tell her, *You know what I found out? Bipolar two is genetic . . .*

"Yeah?" she asks.

"And what the hell does that have to do with me?"

Where, for the first time, things begin to add up.

After that last attempt, in that hospital bed, I suddenly felt the most me I'd felt since childhood, like the high had paused, a ponderous slowing down. It was the tragic familiarity—the smell, the isolation, the petting from sweet West Indian nurses who say I remind them of their daughters, who tell me it will be just fine, the waiting, the time dragging, the many clocks chippering at an invisible speed, the doctor's hmm-hmmming, how the meds create a sound tunnel, the incessant beeping of machines that are supposed to numerate your guarantees, the irony of your heart beating in your ear after you had just tried to kill it, all of this was the tragic irony of everything. I'm ending a past life journey in a movie about ghosts.

It was the fresh beating of my heart I'd tried to kill, and in the process, the many versions of a person I could no longer pretend to be had gone ahead and died instead.

I wanted to be normal my whole life, but I had the wrong ambition. It's in collecting and organizing that we can relocate the erotics of being alive, the gas that keeps any of us going, the drug of seduction, the need to be romanced by what's left of life, to be governed by desire.

Six months into this new treatment, and I'm remembering things I'd blocked out, certain kinds of numerical orientations that once made me happy, word problems that made my brain feel like a brand-new tractor, gassed up and grazing along. I'm doing sixth-grade worksheets in between press releases at work to see what sticks. I'm breaking down fractions and locating their equivalents, I'm calculating the volume and surface of a shape, I'm tabulating ratios and multiplying by 6 and doing long division. Unassisted, my brain is calm enough to parse out one number from the other, I'm simplifying expressions and getting 1 out of 11. I'm hyperaware of the negatives. I'm multiplying and simplifying without a calculator. I'm crying at how easy it always was, how it feels to fly, what it means to be your own tutor and teach yourself a new beginning.

The new therapist tells me to make peace with myself. I start by apologizing for the arrogance of my size, for how I startled him, how I let his love be my field of discovery, the green of his want tortured with the marks of my prancing, how I let self-obsession be an acid that corrodes the denim of a big heavy heart.

This is where the pure, perfect fifth ululates.

As for his lover, she owed me no consideration—and in return I owe her little more than the light whistle of absentia.

On the Blue Line in Chicago, I rush to recover the number of a reporter I should have saved months ago, an important one. My millennial ADHD to blame, technology to suffer it. Did you know, if you've got an iPhone, that voicemails left by blocked numbers get their own little folder, hidden in your log's memory, for you to discover at the least opportune time, a thousand feet above a city that knows nothing about you, almost empty in its winter solitude? I press play on the voicemail from October, it waits patiently for me, his breath precedes him, belabored, drunk. "Camonghne."

That's it. That's the note.

It had been over a year since I'd last dreamt of him in real earnest. I dreamt through it serenely, without sweating from the clutch of his mind on my body, without begging my psyche to wake me. I was dreaming that I was at home again in a Brooklyn or Harlem basement apartment, and I let him across the threshold where he embraced me in arms that seemed bigger and warmer than I remembered them to be. We kissed and I felt relief. In a flicker of scenes we rotate through the rooms of the dream's house, ticking along on the rungs of imaginary time, one second and then one month later, his back to me in plaid, his face to mine in adoration, looks I'd rarely seen, until in one scene I am somehow taller than him and see a great balding spot in the middle of his scalp: gaping, glistening, like the center of his head was a heated pore. When I woke I realized it had been us, an ink, inkizing the blood, killing him.

So. Here's what happened:

All my life I had been waiting for someone to stroke my cheek and cradle my preciousness. I fit in both his hands. I was in pain, and unwell, and he wanted to take care of me, wanted to keep me alive and keep me inside my body. I fell face forward and tucked myself in.

After a while I became neglectful, we were distracted, it was too still a love for me, I needed the friction of evolution, the rub of a higher frequency, but was too coward to admit it, my belly round and well fed. He gave me more than enough and I filled up on it, my ego growing beyond scale and beyond speed. I fed and grew and grew until my need was the size of my shame and my shame was the size of a mountain, where I teetered at the edges of my desire and ignored him with my indecision and my impulses. I fed and watched the color drain from his fingernails, his body begging to be given grace, sucking in the blind of the night at his sores, promising to deserve what he was so full of.

I tried and tried but couldn't do it, failing at the basics of love, the basics of affection, forgetting birthdays and anniversaries, forgetting the shape of his face in the dark. He was begging for my focus, begging me to prioritize my better angels, to deserve him, pulling my teeth out over the sink, pointing at the blood in the mirrors. I was too consumed with my parameters, with the simple ways I'd learned to stay safe, vulnerability a raw performance but not an honest one.

I cheated on him, a lot, with a lot of people, and then I lied about it, and then I gaslit him about it, and then I spent a year cleaning up my own mess, trying to finish the puzzle I'd complicated after I'd lost the pieces, trying to get back to the beginning of the story where it was easy, and I was easy.

And then I asked him to open our relationship as a consolation prize, as if, maybe if another woman could do my work, show him his inherent value and virtue, he wouldn't need to use my body as the proxy for that learning, someone to show him he was indeed beautiful and deserving, and most important, deserving of me. There were rules and guidelines and policies: there was to be nothing serious, he had to do what I had done, fuck without giving away any of the love he'd cultivated in me, hold steady the hegemony of our structure, put me first, make me the sacrosanct of his affection, he had to be strong enough to open up and never give us away, no matter how hungry, how needy.

But I was not attentive enough, giving the caretaking work to another woman hoping she would do just enough to send him back to me in a new shell.

It didn't happen that way, he fell in love with someone who is not me (I maintain to this day it was the idea of her, not the her of her, I don't care what kind of arrogant that makes me) and broke all the rules with someone I deemed radically unworthy, mostly to hurt me but also as a defining mechanism, out of it born a whole glossary of definitions—this is what it means to punish me, to render me small, to make me feel the way he felt, which was much and out of scope.

If he found someone to do all the things I couldn't be bothered with, to do the caretaking I'd never learned, then all the other things I was good at, that made me deserve him, would be primary, and I could just do what I knew and not have to learn skills I could never master: like the ability to love his present self as it was versus the potential I had thought up on his behalf, like the ability to see him at all.

The Math had not mathed at all. I had radically mis-understood him, my own abilities, my true glib desire; I had misrepresented need and given it unfamiliar names,

I had canceled out his access to perform love as I had been taught it, to build a pathway toward something that had always evaded and will always evade me, brought fidelity into a train that was always on its way to a stop.

I lied to him over and over again, murdered his dream of me, and so, in the end, he took himself back, and I realized the blood was the fault of my own cutting, and couldn't imagine continuing to live this way; to live out my own violence on the bodies of the people I want desperately to love and be loved by, to live it out and to fail, so radically, so dangerously, with so much harm around me, not having known that I put myself miles away from the love I desperately want and need, with my inability to see how zero is indivisible, how you welcome in the negatives when you try to give from a well where the water never was and will never be again. I couldn't live this way anymore. So I died.

I am twenty-nine before watching the documentary *Of Two Minds* for the first time. I am struck by how, even in the title, a divisible function is occurring. There are two. There were always two. A thin line between all right and dying. One mind weighing the other out. One mind augmenting the function or malfunction of another.

What I know now is that love is a chaos system dialing us into our highest selves and troubling the foundation of what makes us us. And with a chaos system, all you can control is what you can account for, whatever you can quantify and collect.

I wake in my own bed, wrapped in the chaos of a city I love, tucked into my own arms, and that is sacred. I look in the mirror and there are no doubles, a singular me, and that is sacred. The light dust of the morning is tickling my ear without the interruption of another's breath, and that is sacred. God, through him I learned the most convincing love, the most prosperous, the Christmas tree stacked with our cheap mementos, our affection a sweaty fruit—but what I craved more than anything was the ability to see myself in perpetuity, continuity without burden, the satisfaction of never encountering an empty draft.

Two years of treatment and finally, I know the line. As a test, I'm downloading math worksheets for fifth graders and seeing if I've made enough space in my logic to introduce a new calculus. I'm pushing myself to remember what I loved about tenth-grade precalc, where a five-foot-five Mr. Anderson handed a copy of *Einstein's Dreams* to me and helped me see how numbers become shapes, and how shapes become functions, and how functions become systems, and how systems can be disrupted. If I know the line, then I know its function. And if I break the function, the system cannot survive.

I crave a kiss and kiss myself.

Three years later, over samosas and lunchtime chicken marsala,

Mommy and I laugh at the pinkness of Trump from the television above our heads. Massaging my hand, Mom begins to tear up a bit.

What? I ask, eyeing her suspiciously.

"You're just so . . . you!" The smile we share skins across her face as she grabs mine. "And you're okay. I spent so many years just not knowing . . . if you would ever . . . if my baby would ever . . ."

She wipes her tears and flips her dreads over one shoulder, the solemn pride dressing our table. I know what she means. I rub her hand with my thumb, slightly embarrassed by her emoting.

She palms my face, a sweetness from her I hadn't known in years. "I'm just glad you're back."

I roll my eyes, shying away from it.

Ancient Pythagoreans subscribed to the dogma of trans-migration and memory, both of which they believed to be the key to a soulful immortality, an immortality only attainable if the soul takes a three-thousand-year journey in which your individual soul inhabits many different bodies in order to return to the divine. It's this insistence on remembering that allows one to rise with the gods, a cumulative accounting of three thousand years of wisdom, a collection that improves the soul and magnifies its offering to all beings.

Sometimes a benign heartbreak is meaningful. Sometimes it sums up to nothing. Who's to know? And does it matter? It's the abacus of your growth, how many inches up from the ground you've gotten charted.

At the coffee shop, an interested man observes me in silence, then asks me what I'm working on when I take my headphones off to thank the waiter. He's kind of my type, but I'm weary now, and he thinks I don't see him. But I do. I tell him I'm working on a book. "Oh yeah, a book?" he croons, smiling like I made a joke. "What's your book about?"

Heartbreak . . . romance . . . that kind of stuff.

"That's it," he asks, "heartbreak?"

That's it, I say. *Just heartbreak.*

Black girls get to write about benign heartbreak too. Proud and saccharine and pathetic.

When you're healed you tell the story differently.

I loved a man so hard it made me sick.

I loved myself so hard I brought her back.

In an article that lists "15 Crazy Instances of Self-Similarity," I see nature performing a kind of humanness. First, I evaluate whether or not what I think I see is what I see or if my human eyes assume a supremacy.

The article shows pictures of spirals in nature, in whirlpools, in sand dunes, in ringworm infections, in space. In some spirals, there is momentum and force; in others, just patterns.

When I spiral, things around me become their own spirals, taking on their own momentum, taking on their own force, fractals of my many fractals taking on their own diameters—echoes billowing in neon rings, sonic abstraction in the mind of a maestro. To see it is to see it.

Maybe it's an algorithm. Maybe it's me. I hate the article, but I love what I'm starting to know.

The body is playing its part in the story of my soul. This body, and each one of the small terrors that break my heart, every single one.

All the time now, as I'm stirring tea in the steam of the morning, I think of my mom telling me that the shortest distance between two destinations is a straight line.

I'm ten—she's at the stove aggressively stirring an okra and cornmeal mixture that she'll use to make fungi. She takes a pause to cut vegetables, pushing a cutting board and a knife toward me at the opposite end of the table, gesturing for me to follow her lead.

Things are going to be very hard for you, she says to me, stripping the potato of its skin—metathetic, processional. I pick up a potato too. I go at its flesh.

Things are going to be hard for you because your brain works differently from other people's. Know that now. There's nothing wrong with you. Something happened to you that changed your chemistry and now your brain is different. Do you understand what I mean? She looks up at me out of the side of her eye as she shaves another layer of the potato. I nod yes.

I need you to understand this, she says. *No one is going to work as hard as I do to understand what makes you different. Nobody has to care about what hurts you because that's not their job. It's not the world's job to understand you, it's your job to understand the world. And the more you understand it, the more you learn how to get around it. The more you understand it, the more you understand who you can trust and how far you can stretch. You cannot wait for them to understand you, or they will kill you. You have to do it.*

Do you understand? She drops the potatoes into the boiling water, stretching her arm out behind her to keep me at arm's distance from the stove, a reminder that the water is hot and that I am small.

I'm sorry, but you have to show the work, she says. *You have to do it yourself. Do you understand me?* she asks.

Yes. I understand.

Things are almost back to some normalcy when I meet a man who has the potential to trigger something enormous in me. He is kind and fatherly and protective and I recognize that it's a test. It takes five months for the flags to show themselves, and just when they do, he disappears like a drop of water on a line. It stings for a while, but it doesn't overwhelm me. I can feel every part of what it does to my body, and I feel stable in feeling it, more in awe of what my new coping mechanisms allow me than I am with how bad it feels. A couple of years later, he reappears and the Pattern app on my phone lets me know that I am at the end of a cycle. I know by just knowing that this is my soul remembering, poking.

And it was just like this the first time we fucked, the stars blown out and the bourbon as dry as a whistle. I always walk in unassumingly. For an hour, we talk about his ego. It takes three hours for me to remember what it is that spun me around about him in the first place. It takes one hour to work up the courage to ask how we got here. To ask if he knows. Ultimately, he doesn't. He tells me there are two trains and two separate sets of tracks and how could he have known where I was going? It's true. We aren't a caboose. So I park and fish out the memory box. I wave my hands about a bit and find a dimple in the structure. There was a time where I fit so small. And that small dimple held me. Not traumatic, not benign, he fished me out and he escaped my size. But I stayed haunted by his.

I step away from the box with all this new information and now I know at least how I got there and back here again. I look across at him in his arrogant discomfort and I want to hug it. Its familiarity makes me feel haunted and free. Sometimes a small star is a supernova and it happens at the most inconvenient time. Sometimes the inconvenience is a speak. For instance, I know who I am now and that makes it harder for him to call me *baby*. I know who I am now and that makes it harder to reach back behind himself for my hand. He's the king of his castle and I'm the king of mine. Isn't it weird to see two castles casting shadows on each other? He's intrigued but uncomfortable at how I grew so big, so fast. He keeps saying he wants something deeper, a connection, to be partnered, but I don't know who he is talking to because he can't look me in the eye.

Anyway now we are laughing again because isn't it all hilarious? And we both have to pee, and it's cold, so let's just go where we know. His place. Which has gained a sense of casual commotion. It's too lived-in, not finessed enough. When he first moved here, I could hear myself cum and it would echo. Now, the plants are in the way. It feels the same and also foreign. I'm a mystery to him and he is almost the same, except when he softens it feels performative, and I couldn't see through him more clearly. Sometimes a small boy becomes a big man and his hands fail to grow in. I'm facedown over his lap as he palms the plums of my ass and it's too much flesh for him. It's too fat, he can't hold it. His small hands look comical as they grip at me. Years ago, every part of me fit wherever he placed me. He likes that I'm thick, but the good part is that none of it is for him. I just am this momentous, this large, and I'm not even trying.

He grabs at my face, squeezing hard when he kisses me, trying to remind me of our places, relative to each other, but the system is outdated. It doesn't turn me on like it used to, his dominance. It's not that it's contrived, it just doesn't stand up when the lights are on and he can see me clearly (which is new, him seeing me). I'm tempted, mostly for old times' sake, and because I know what I'm getting, which at some point satisfied me, but now I can't know for sure, because I am so much more sufficient, and I don't need his affirmation to orgasm. It's almost useless. Which exhausts my purpose here. It's not the same anymore, and I have nothing to prove.

So I suck on his soft lips a little more, biting at the flesh, feeling him get worked up, feeling him remember what he loves about being inside me. Then I call my Uber, because it's late, and because I would rather be talking to my best friend, giggling over a cigarette.

And there it is. That's the math. I want to be elsewhere, so I go. There's nothing here for me that can't be duped, that I can't find elsewhere, in a less poisonous container, so I leave.

It's that simple these days. It was never this simple before.

My train leaves the station, and there is no regret. It was a rest stop anyway. A place to stretch the legs. A way to check the compass. I was there then, and I'm here now. Look at me, look at how I do this.

Look at how I count the truth, and change my mind.

A fractal is a never-ending pattern—infinitely complex. It's a simple equation processed over and over again, reproducing itself in perpetuity, in everything, hiding around us and inside of us, like Russian dolls or a forest bordered by and stuffed full with the trees of its own soil, a river that splits and meets itself in the mouth of another river. A simple equation processed over and over again, like a stamp, like your DNA, like your brain, like your lungs, like a mother.

I've been curious lately about how the self reproduces itself within itself, its patterns permuting and duplicating in foreign systems, like fractals do, like the Mandelbrot set, never ending—the fingerprint of God.

Herr God, Herr Lucifer
Beware
Beware.

NOTES

On page 116, selection borrowed from T. S. Eliot's "The Love Song of J. Alfred Prufrock."

On page 152, selection borrowed from William Shakespeare's *Macbeth*.

On page 219, selection borrowed from Sylvia Plath's "Lady Lazarus."

Throughout, I reference philosopher Dr. James Luchte's research on Pythagoras and transmigration in the Pythagorean religion, from his book *Pythagoras and the Doctrine of Transmigration: Wandering Souls* (Bloomsbury, 2009).

ACKNOWLEDGMENTS

To my agent, Alice, who knows my voice, what it can do, and how to protect it. Your support has been life-changing.

To my editor, Nicole, for seeing *Dyscalculia* and for allowing it to become what it became.

To artist GB Kim, my best thought partner, my dearest friend—once again, our brains have made good trouble. Thank you for your art, and for making the cover come to life.

To my family, immediate and extended, for holding me and for not holding any of this against me.

To X, for the lesson of a lifetime. I'm forever different because of our story.

To everyone at One World, for the love, care, and labor put into getting this book to our readers.

To an endless list of mentors and friends who gave feed-back, critical thoughts, blurbs, and much encouragement.

To my readers, for choosing to step onto this algedonic ride and stay till the end. I hope it was worth it.

ABOUT THE AUTHOR

CAMONGHNE FELIX, poet and essayist, is the author of *Build Yourself a Boat,* which was longlisted for the 2019 National Book Award in Poetry and shortlisted for the PEN/Open Book Award and a Lambda Literary Award. Her poetry has appeared in or is forthcoming from the Academy of American Poets website, *Freeman's, Harvard Review, LitHub, The New Yorker,* PEN America, *Poetry Magazine,* and elsewhere. Her essays have been featured in *Vanity Fair, New York, Teen Vogue,* and other publications.

Twitter: @camonghne
Instagram: @camonghne